C000175491

بسم الله الرحمن الرحيم

ربنا

Rabbanā

Supplications from the Holy Qurʾān Accompanied by Arabic Text with English Translation

Compiled by

Abul Hussain

with a Foreword by

Malik Badri

Recitation by

Muhammad Jebril

ISBN: 978-0-9932717-0-0

Published by Alif Recordings
PO BOX 50514
London E14 7WP
www.alifrecordings.com

Qur'ān Translation	Sahih International
Project Supervisor, Arabic Translation, Hadith Referencing	Ahmed Keeris
Audio Mastering & Executive Producer	Abul Hussain
English Narration	Mahmoud Taji
Cover design	Syed Dohan Nuh
Typesetting	www.scholarlytype.com

Acknowledgements
Asma Begum, Ahmed Keeris,
Shaykh Muzaffar Noori, and Ehsan Abdullah Hannan

British Library Cataloguing-in-Publication Data
A catalogue record for this book is available from the British Library.
Rabbanā: Supplications from the Holy Qur'ān accompanied
by Arabic Text with English Translation

Printed in the United Kingdom

Distribution for UK, Europe & International
Darussalam
Leyton Business Centre

Unit 17 Etloe Road	+44 (0) 20 8539 4885
Leyton	sales@darussalam.com
London E10 7BT	www.darussalam.com

For our beloved daughter

Maryam Hannah Hussain

May God, Most High, provide mercy, protection and guidance throughout her journey in life, Āmīn

TRANSLITERATION KEY

Arabic	Transliteration	Arabic	Transliteration
ا	a	ظ	ẓ
ب	b	ع	ʿ
ت	t	غ	gh
ث	th	ف	f
ج	j	ق	q
ح	ḥ	ك	k
خ	kh	ل	l
د	d	م	m
ذ	dh	ن	n
ر	r	هـ	h
ز	z	ء	ʾ
س	s	ة	a or at or atan
ش	sh	و	w
ص	ṣ	ى	y
ض	ḍ	يّ	iyy (final form ī)
ط	ṭ	آ	ā

Arabic glyph	English meaning	Usage
عز وجل	Mighty and Majestic is He	On mention of God
عليه السلام عليهم السلام	Peace be upon him / them	On mention of one or more angles or prophets
سبحانه وتعالى	Exalted and Most High	On mention of God
صلى الله عليه وسلم	May the peace and blessings of God be upon him	On mention of the Prophet
رضي الله عنه رضي الله عنهم	May God be pleased with him / them	On mention of one or more companions of the Prophet
رضي الله عنها	May God be pleased with her	On mention of a female companion of the Prophet

CONTENTS

FOREWORD

Supplication, or *duʿāʾ*, has always been revered as one of the noblest forms of worship. In the authentic *ḥadīth, duʿāʾ* is described as true worship or *ʿibāda*. The noble Qurʾān calls on us to remember man's utter dependence upon his Lord. God, Most High, is *Rabb al-ʿĀlamīn,* the Lord of the worlds. He is Lord of mankind, jinn, and all that exists; nothing occurs except by His leave. Unfortunately, this conviction is weak in our hearts; we are busy pursuing our lives, heedless of our eternal reliance on the Creator. We only find ourselves truly supplicating for divine intervention when our own limited abilities inevitably fail us. It is in such situations that we truly experience humility, awe, and absolute submission to God, Most High. Yet when He reaches out to us many of us regress and forget the greatness of supplication. We find a most potent parable from God, Most High, in the noble Qurʾān:

> *And when they board a ship, they supplicate God, sincere to Him in religion. But when He delivers them to the land, at once they associate others with Him* (al-ʿAnkabūt, 29:65).

As Muslims, we worship none other than God, Most High; Him alone do we ask for help. However, we often forget that He alone controls our destiny and, unthinkingly, we look elsewhere for our sustenance. We find ourselves in the hands of our employers, our governments or others who possess authority over us; we thus remain unaware of the spiritual hazard we fall into when relying upon anyone or anything other than God, Most High. Refuge from such a situation can be found only in sincere *duʿāʾ*. Through supplication we can become spiritually conscious of the power God, Most High, has over our affairs. Only then can we feel His love and mercy and, ultimately, experience *khushūʿ*.

Khushūʿ is typically translated as "submission," a term that hardly does such a concept justice. In reality there can be no adequate translation for this Islamic term. One can fully submit to a person of authority but it is unlikely that one will feel even the slightest affection for such a figure. *Khushūʿ* entails a submission to God, Most High, out of both love (*maḥabba)* and fear of Him (*taqwā*), it stems from a never-ending hope in His response. It is through supplication that we reach this dynamic spiritual feeling that God, Most High, wishes His slaves to have for Him.

God, Most High, made supplication obligatory upon his servants; a Muslim performing his or her five daily prayers typically supplicates numerous times daily. Supplication is a fundamental part of our worship.

May God, Most High, bless the author, Abul Hussain, for writing this book and for honouring me to write its foreword. It is of great value to many, especially Muslims in the West.

Professor Malik Badri

Holder of the Chair of Ibn Khaldun,
International Islamic University Malaysia
Distinguished Professor of Psychology,
Ahfad University, Omdurman, Sudan

INTRODUCTION

IN THE NAME OF God, the most Merciful, the Beneficent. Indeed, all praise belongs to God alone, the Lord of the universe. We seek His help and forgiveness. We seek refuge with God from the evil within ourselves and our bad deeds, for whoever God guides will never be led astray, and whoever God leaves astray, none can guide. I bear witness that there is none worthy of worship but God, alone, who has no partner; and I bear witness that Muḥammad is His servant and Messenger, may the ever abundant salutations, peace, and blessings of God be upon him, his family, and companions.

The Importance, Benefits, and Excellence of *Duʿāʾ*

Duʿāʾ means supplication or invocation. It is the calling out, and seeking of aid from God, the All-Knowing and the All-Hearing, for the fulfilment of one's needs and the acknowledgement and appreciation of His majesty, eminence, and governance over His creation. It is a state of humility that emanates from the heart of the believer, who is weak and helpless, and cannot achieve anything without the help and aid of God ﷻ. The attestation of *duʿāʾ* is the complete submission to God ﷻ and His absolute right to be worshipped (*tawḥīd al-ulūhiyya*).[1] It brings out the right status of man: that he is created needy, without any control over his affairs, rather he is the one that is controlled. He is in need of his Creator in every instant, while God ﷻ remains independent of need from His creation. Man is in need of continual guidance from his Lord.

Duʿāʾ is a noble act in the sight of God ﷻ. The Messenger of God ﷺ beautifully stated this when he said, "There is nothing nobler in the sight of God than *duʿāʾ*."[2] *Duʿāʾ* is worship.[3] The best form of worship is *duʿāʾ*[4] and it is one of the most powerful and effective acts of worship a human being can engage in. This is reflected in the worshipper's repentance for his sins, his acceptance of a state of humility, awe, and fear before His Lord, and his submission to the will of God ﷻ. He raises his hands and turns to God with the best of hopes of being answered, and earnestly desires reward and respite from Him. If God ﷻ intends good for His servant, He will open doors of repentance (*tawba*) and remorse for him. From His mercy (*raḥma*) He will facilitate an approach towards Him. The supplicant longs to obtain from His Lord the contentment (*riḍā*), peace, serenity and beneficence that he cannot find elsewhere. This is regarded as a mark of servitude (*ʿubūdīyya*) and is characteristic of human submission, and at the same time a demonstration of the Omnipotence and Lordliness (*rabbāniyya*) of God ﷻ.

Duʿāʾ is a way of making a connection with God ﷻ at any time and in any place. The believers call upon God frequently throughout the day and night. *Duʿāʾ* can be made for the individual, the family, friends, strangers, those in dire circumstances, for the believers, and even for the whole of humanity. When making *duʿāʾ* it is acceptable to ask for good in this worldly life and in the hereafter (*ākhira*). A person making

1 Ibn Taymiyya, *Kitāb al-Īmān*.

2 Aḥmad, al-Tirmidhī, al-Ḥākim, and others.

3 Aḥmad.

4 al-Ḥākim.

duʿāʾ should not hold back, but ask God ﷻ to grant requests, regardless of their importance because He is fully capable of granting anything. This ability of God ﷻ is expressly found in Sūra Ghāfir: *He is the Ever-Living; there is no deity except Him, so call upon Him, [be] sincere to Him in religion. [All] praise is [due] to God, Lord of the worlds* (40:65).[5]

The generosity of God ﷻ to his creation is also found in the *ḥadīth* in which the Messenger of God ﷺ said, "When one of you asks for something [from God], then let him [ask] abundantly, for indeed he is asking his Lord."

The Messenger of God ﷺ encouraged believers to read *duʿāʾ*, he said: "The supplication of a Muslim for his brother in his absence will certainly be answered. Every time he makes a supplication for good for his brother, the angel appointed for this particular task says: Āmīn! May it be for you, too."[6] Although making *duʿāʾ* is not an obligation, there are many benefits to it. Sincere *duʿāʾ* promotes a feeling of closeness to God ﷻ that increases faith, gives hope and relief to the distressed, and saves the supplicant from despair and isolation. A further motivation for making *duʿāʾ* is found in the following *ḥadīths*.[7] The Messenger of God ﷺ said, "Verily, the person who does not ask God, God becomes angry at him,"[8] and furthermore, "Verily your Lord is One, Modest and Generous, and when His servant raises his hands to Him in supplication, He is hesitant to return them empty."[9] Throughout the Qurʾān, God ﷻ encourages the believer to call on Him, as He asks us to make known our hopes, fears, and uncertainties and to be assured that He listens to every word uttered.

---

5 Translations from the Qurʾān are from the Sahih International Edition.

6 Muslim.

7 The reports of sayings, actions, and approvals of the Prophet Muḥammad ﷺ

8 al-Tirmidhī.

9 Abū Dāwūd, Aḥmad, and al-Tirmidhī.

And your Lord says, "Call upon Me; I will respond to you." Indeed, those who disdain My worship will enter Hell [rendered] contemptible (Ghāfir, 40:60).

Say, "O My servants who have transgressed against themselves [by sinning], do not despair of the mercy of God. Indeed, God forgives all sins. Indeed, it is He who is the Forgiving, the Merciful" (al-Zumar, 39:53).

Say, "Call upon God or call upon the Most Merciful [al-Raḥmān]. Whichever [name] you call—to Him belong the best names." And do not recite [too] loudly in your prayer or [too] quietly but seek between that an intermediate way (al-Isrāʾ, 17:110).

And when My servants ask you, [O Muḥammad], concerning Me—indeed I am near. I respond to the invocation of the supplicant when he calls upon Me. So let them respond to Me [by obedience] and believe in Me that they may be [rightly] guided (al-Baqara, 2:186).

The Prerequisites of *Duʿāʾ*

Because *duʿāʾ* is worship, it is important to be aware of the preconditions that are necessary for one's *duʿāʾ* to be accepted.

The Realisation that Only God Responds to *Duʿāʾ*

Is He [not best] who responds to the desperate one when he calls upon Him and removes evil and makes you inheritors of the earth? Is there a deity with God? Little do you remember (al-Naml, 27:62).

The Importance of Sincerity in Making *Duʿāʾ* to God Alone

Is it other than God you would invoke, if you should be truthful? (al-Anʿām, 6:40).

And those you call upon besides Him are unable to help you, nor can they help themselves (al-Aʿrāf, 7:197).

The sincerity in *duʿāʾ* is explicitly expressed in Sūra Ghāfir: *He is the Ever-Living; there is no deity except Him, so call upon Him, [being] sincere to Him in religion. [All] praise is [due] to God, Lord of the worlds* (40:65).

A reminder of this is found in the advice given by the Messenger of God ﷺ to Ibn ʿAbbās ؓ when he said, "Be mindful of God and God will protect you. Be mindful of God and you will find Him in front of you. If you ask, then ask God [alone]; and if you seek help, then seek help from God [alone]."[10]

The Correct Way to Perform *Tawassul*

Tawassul is the act of seeking help from God ﷻ by performing certain acts to increase one's chances of the *duʿāʾ* being accepted. The concept of *tawassul* is one of the most important etiquettes of *duʿāʾ*, and one of the greatest considerations that increase the chances of a *duʿāʾ* being accepted. Some people who misunderstand this concept may fall into *shirk* (associating partners with God) or *bidʿa* (innovation in the creed or in acts of worship). Linguistically, *tawassul* means to come closer to an objective and to gain proximity to a desired goal or outcome. In Islamic terms, it signifies the act of trying to come closer to God ﷻ through manners that have been prescribed by the Qurʾān and

10 al-Tirmidhī, in *The 40 Ḥadīth of Imām al-Nawawī*, also known as *Arbaʿīn*.

prophetic Sunna. In sum, it is a means of seeking nearness to God ﷻ. *O you who have believed, fear God and seek the* <u>*means*</u> *[of nearness] to Him and strive in His cause that you may succeed* (al-Māʾida, 5:35). These acts may include mentioning God's names and attributes, acknowledging God's blessings and favours, being in a state (i.e., of poverty, deprivation, humility or shortcomings) before God, mentioning the good deeds one has done, or asking another person to make *duʿāʾ* for you (but without abandoning one's own *duʿāʾ* and without relying only on others).

A great example of using one's good deeds in *tawassul* is found in the following narration of ʿAbdallāh b. ʿUmar b. al-Khaṭṭāb ؓ who heard the Messenger of God ﷺ say:

> Three men among those who came before you set out until night came and they reached a cave, so they entered it. A rock fell down from the mountain and blocked the entrance of the cave. They said: "Nothing will save you from this unless you supplicate to God by virtue of a righteous deed you have done." Thereupon, one of them said: "O God! I had parents who were old, and I used to offer them milk before any of my children or slaves. One day I went far away in search of pasture [for my herds] and did not come back until after they had slept. When I milked as usual and brought the drink I found them both asleep. I hated to disturb them and also disliked to give milk to my children before them. My children were crying out of hunger at my feet but I waited with the bowl in my hand for them to wake up. When they awoke at dawn, they drank the milk. O God! If I did so to seek Your pleasure, then deliver us from the distress caused by the rock." The rock moved slightly but they were unable to escape.
>
> The next said: "O God! I had a cousin whom I loved more than anyone else (in another version: as passionately as any man can

love a woman). I wanted to have sexual intercourse with her but she refused. Hard pressed in a year of famine, she approached me. I gave her one hundred and twenty dinars on condition that she would yield herself to me. She agreed and when we got together (for sexual intercourse), she said: Fear God and do not break the seal unlawfully. I moved away from her in spite of the fact that I loved her most passionately; and I let her keep the money I had given her. O God! If I did that to seek Your pleasure, then remove the distress we are in." The rock moved aside a bit further but they were still unable to get out.

The third one said: "O God! I hired some labourers and paid them their wages, except one, who departed without taking his due. I invested his money in business and the business prospered greatly. After a long time, he came to me and said: O slave of God! Pay me my dues. I said: All that you see is yours—camels, cattle, goats, and slaves. He said: O slave of God! Do not mock me. I assured him that I was not joking. So he took all the things and went away. He spared nothing. O God! If I did so seeking Your pleasure, then relieve us of our distress." The rock slipped aside and they left and walked away freely.[11]

There is also a form of *tawassul* that is prohibited. We must be careful not to perform *tawassul* using the honour of the creation, or their righteousness, personality, rank or glory, whether they are from the prophets or *ṣaliḥīn* (righteous people), and we must not perform *tawassul* by attending graves and pleading to its dead inhabitants. We learn from Sūra Fāṭir (35:22), that we cannot make the dead in the graves hear us, while in Sūrat al-Aḥqāf (46:5), God addresses those who seek their aid as being "further astray." According to Ibn Taymiyya, taking angels and prophets as intermediaries and calling upon and relying on them for

11 al-Bukhārī and Muslim.

benefit and the removal of harm makes one, by the consensus (*ijmāʿ*) of the Muslim community, an unbeliever.[12] Despite this and out of ignorance some people make *duʿāʾ* by saying, "O God by the right of your Prophet...," or "by the right of the sacred house...forgive me," or "O God by the right of the *awliyāʾ* and the pious, etc...," and "O God by the honour of the men of God, and by the honour of those in whose presence we are and under whose assistance we exist, relieve us and the distressed from all distress..." We should instead reject this and direct our worship to God ﷻ alone, the blessed and Most High, the One who controls harm and benefit, in His hand is the governance and protection of everything. According to Ibn Kathīr, the great Qurʾān commentator, we must seek to draw near to God ﷻ by obedience to Him and through actions that are pleasing to Him.[13]

The Importance of Avoiding Haste

Performing *duʿāʾ* in haste causes it to be rejected, as indicated in the following narration of Abū Hurayra رضي الله عنه, in which the Messenger of God ﷺ said, "The *duʿāʾ* of any worshipper will continue to receive a response, as long as he does not ask for a sin or break the ties of kinship, and as long as he is not hasty." It was then asked, "O Messenger of God, what does it mean to be hasty?" He ﷺ responded, "A worshipper says, 'I have prayed and prayed, and I do not see that it will be accepted,' so he gives up hope of being answered, and leaves *duʿāʾ*."[14] Making *duʿāʾ* should also be continuous and one should avoid giving up simply because it has not been answered (or the response is delayed). The Messenger of God ﷺ said, "You will receive a response as long as you

12 Ibn Taymiyya, *Wāsiṭa bayn al-ḥaqq wa-l-khālq.*

13 For a detailed discussion on this refer to Muhammad Naasir ud-Deen al-Albaani, *Tawassul: Its Types and Its Rulings.*

14 Abū Dāwūd, Aḥmad, al-Tirmidhī, and al-Ḥākim.

are not hasty…"[15] We must also understand that whatever God ﷻ decides or decrees for us it is always good (Āl ʿImrān, 3:19) and that afflictions are a test from God ﷻ to draw us closer to Him. The Messenger of God ﷺ indicated this by saying, "The greatness of a reward is based on the severity of the trial. And if God loves a person, He tests him, so whoever is pleased [with God], then he will have the pleasure [of God], but whoever is angry, then he will receive the anger [of God]."[16] Ibn Qayyim reminds us that the more we are able to believe in the rewards that await us, the easier it becomes to have patience.[17] We must therefore endeavour to have perseverance.

The Importance of Good Intentions

Duʿāʾ should always be made with the best of intentions with a clear and beneficial objective. For example, one might ask for an increase in wealth that is related to his intention to spend more on his relatives and the poor, and so increase rewards and good deeds. Similarly if one reads *duʿāʾ* to marry a pious woman, it could be linked to an intention to avoid falling into prohibited (*ḥarām*) acts and instead start a pious family. An example of this can found in the *ḥadīth* of Abū Dāwūd, whereby the Messenger of God ﷺ said: "When a person comes to visit the sick, then let him say, 'O God! Cure your servant so-and-so, for he will then inflict a wound on an enemy, or walk for your sake to the prayer." Here the purpose of curing those from sickness could be so they may aid the religion. Good intentions should also be linked to one's sincerity (*ikhlāṣ*), which is at the root of God's acceptance of our deeds and actions (*aʿmāl*) ﷻ. The very centrality of it is demonstrated in the first *ḥadīth* of the forty *ḥadīth* in al-Nawawī's collection (*Arbaʿīn*). In a

15 al-Bukhārī, Muslim, Abū Dāwūd, and others.

16 al-Tirmidhī and Ibn Māja.

17 Ibn Qayyim al-Jawziyya, *Patience and Gratitude: An abridged translation of ʿUddat al-ṣābirīn wa-dhakhīrat al-shākirīn.*

famous report, the Messenger of God ﷺ said: "Actions are according to intentions..." (*innama al-aʿmālu bi-niyāt*). This core *ḥadīth* and the primary premise of having the right intention is at the forefront of any righteous action (*aʿmāl ṣāliḥāt*); this is further reinforced in Sūrat al-Anʿām: *Say, "Indeed, my prayer, my rites of sacrifice, my living and my dying are for God, Lord of the worlds"* (6:162).

Making *Duʿāʾ* of a Pure and Good Nature

The wording of the *ḥadīth* narrated by Abū Hurayra ؓ: "... as long as he does not ask for a sin or break the ties of kinship..."[18] is a clear demonstration that *duʿāʾ* must not contain anything that is not permitted in Islam or that which leads to an evil outcome. In another account the Messenger of God ﷺ said, "Do not make *duʿāʾ* against yourself, nor make *duʿāʾ* against your children, nor your property, for your *duʿāʾ* may coincide with the time when God grants supplication, and your *duʿāʾ* might be granted [and cause you harm]."[19]

The Importance of an Attentive Heart

One must be aware that *duʿāʾ* should be made with mindfulness and presence of the heart (*ḥuḍūr al-qalb*), and know that the plea is being made to God, the Lord of honour. It is not befitting to make *duʿāʾ* in a neglectful way, by repeating words meaninglessly and without conscious effort, appreciation or feeling. One should also be confident and certain that the *duʿāʾ* will be accepted. The Messenger of God ﷺ said, "Make *duʿāʾ* to God in a state of certainty, [knowing] that your *duʿāʾ* will receive a response, and know that God does not respond

18 Abū Dāwūd, Aḥmad, al-Tirmidhī, and al-Ḥākim.

19 Muslim.

to a *duʿāʾ* that comes from a negligent and inattentive heart."[20] The Messenger of God ﷺ also said, "Let not any one of you say, 'O God, forgive me if You will, O God, have mercy on me if You will.' Let him be resolute in the matter, while knowing that no one can compel God to do anything."[21] According to Ibn Qayyim,[22] the heart can become sick like the physical body; its cure lies in seeking forgiveness and protection. It can also accumulate rust, like that of a mirror; unless it is polished with the remembrance (*dhikr*) of God ﷻ. We are then encouraged to be actively engaged in the *duʿāʾ* and conscious of our inner state (*ḥāl*).

The Purifying of One's Sustenance

The necessary condition of any *duʿāʾ* relies upon the purity and lawfulness of one's food. Abū Hurayra ؓ narrated that the Messenger of God ﷺ said, "O people! God is al-Ṭayyib [Pure], and He only accepts that which is pure! God has commanded the believers what he has commanded the messengers, for He said, 'Messengers! Eat from the pure foods, and do right.' He ﷺ added, 'O you who believe! Eat from the pure and good foods We have given you.' The Messenger of God ﷺ then mentioned a traveller on a long journey; he is dishevelled and dusty, and then stretches forth his hands to the sky, saying, 'O my Lord! O my Lord!'—while his food is unlawful, his drink is unlawful, his clothes are unlawful, and he is nourished unlawfully; how can he be answered?"[23] Pure sustenance (*rizq ṭayyib*) goes hand in hand with *taqwā* (fearing God and consciousness of Him) and is also an essential quality of the heart. Umm Salama ؓ narrated that the Messenger of God ﷺ used to say after *fajr* prayer, *Allāhumma innī asʾaluka ʿilmān nāfiʿan, wa rizqan ṭayyiban, wa ʿamalan mutaqabbalan* ("O God, I

20 al-Tirmidhī and al-Ḥākim.

21 al-Bukhārī and Muslim.

22 Ibn Qayyim al-Jawziyya, *al-Fawāʾid.*

23 Aḥmad, Muslim, and al-Tirmidhī.

ask You for beneficial knowledge, goodly provision and acceptable deeds").[24] In Sūrat al-Māiʾda (5:27) it is mentioned, "Indeed, God only accepts [*duʿāʾ*] from the righteous [who fear Him]." Therefore, we must be careful what we eat and drink and examine the sources of our earnings and sustenance.

Saying Prayers for the Messenger of God ﷺ

It is recommended that when making *duʿāʾ*, we accompany it with prayers (*al-ṣalat ʿala al-nabī*) for the Messenger of God ﷺ. For he ﷺ has said: "When any one of you makes *duʿāʾ*, let him start by glorifying his Lord and praising Him, then let him send blessings upon the Prophet, then let him pray for whatever he wants."[25] In another tradition, the Messenger of God ﷺ said, "Every *duʿāʾ* is covered until [the person] prays for the Prophet."[26] Here the term 'covered' means it is not raised up to God ﷻ until it is accompanied by prayer for the Messenger of God ﷺ. ʿUmar رضي الله عنه said: "*Duʿāʾ* is detained between the heavens and the earth and no part of it is taken up until you send blessings for your Prophet."[27] However, this is not a necessary condition for every *duʿāʾ* to be accepted, but rather a recommendation. The Messenger of God ﷺ instructed his companions on other occasions to read *duʿāʾ*, whereby accompanying prayers for the Prophet was not mentioned.[28]

Not only is the prayer for the Messenger of God ﷺ recited in conjunction with *duʿāʾ*, but by themselves they can bring about more blessings and protection from God ﷻ. The Messenger of God ﷺ said, "A messenger came to me from my Lord and said, 'There is no worshipper who prays for you, except that God will pray for him ten times!' A man

---

24 Ibn Māja and Aḥmad.

25 al-Tirmidhī.

26 al-Nasāʾī.

27 al-Tirmidhī.

28 Abu Ammaar Yasir Qadhi, *Duʿāʾ: The Weapon of the Believer.*

then stood up and said, 'O Messenger of God! Should I make half of my prayers for you?' He ﷺ replied, 'if you wish.' He then asked, 'Should I make two-thirds of my prayers for you?' He ﷺ replied, 'if you wish.' He then asked, 'Should I make all of my prayers for you?' He ﷺ replied, 'In that case, God would suffice you in your needs of this world and the hereafter!'"[29] In another similar narration, the Messenger of God ﷺ responded to questions about sending prayers for him with, "then your worries will be taken care of and sins will be forgiven."[30] Invoking blessings for him ﷺ holds great reward for the supplicant. The superiority of sending praise for the Messenger of God ﷺ and his status is noted in Sūrat al-Aḥzāb (33:56): "Indeed, God confers blessing upon the Prophet, and His angels [ask Him to do so]. O you who have believed, ask [God to confer] blessing upon him and ask [God to grant him] peace."

Balancing *Duʿāʾ* and Other Daily Obligations

One must prioritise what needs to be done in life. Worship can be divided into two categories: *Ṣalāt*, that which has a specific time, and *duʿāʾ*, that which can be done at any time. *Duʿāʾ* should not be performed at the expense of obligatory prayers. The place of *duʿāʾ* and obligatory matters are illustrated in a *ḥadīth* and in *al-Adab al-Mufrad* of al-Bukhārī, whereby the Messenger of God ﷺ narrated the story of Jurayj al-ʿAbid, a monk who chose to pray instead of answering his mother's numerous calls; he could have shortened it, but did not, and this resulted in his mother making *duʿāʾ* against him. As a consequence he faced social humiliation and abuse from his community, before his original status of dignity and honour was restored. This short story has lessons for us: *Duʿāʾ* must not be given a higher status than other matters which should not be delayed. After one responds to obligatory matters,

29 al-Tirmidhī.

30 al-Tirmidhī.

one is free to make *duʿāʾ*. It is narrated by Abū Hurayra ﷺ, that the Messenger of God ﷺ said: "Three supplications are answered, without doubt: the invocation of a parent against his son, the supplication of a traveller, and the supplication of the oppressed."[31]

Deeds are only accepted if sincere and according to the Sunna. In *Iʿlām al-muwwaqiʿīn* Ibn Qayyim al-Jawziyya discusses the essential criteria which determine if our deeds are ultimately accepted by God ﷻ. He reports that al-Fuḍayl b. ʿIyāḍ said, "God purifies good deeds and makes them correct. Indeed, if deeds are sincere and incorrect, they will not be accepted. If deeds are correct and insincere, they will not be accepted; they are only accepted if they are both sincere and correct. Sincere means they are done for God ﷻ alone and correct means they are done according to the Sunna." Then he recited the verse, *So whoever hopes in the meeting with his Lord, let him work righteousness and associate none in the worship of his Lord* (al-Kahf, 18:110).

Our guide is the Messenger of God ﷺ and his teachings direct us to the straight path, as God ﷻ, says, *And indeed, [O Muḥammad], you guide to a straight path* (al-Shūrā, 42:52).

This guidance is further strengthened: *Say, [O Muḥammad], "If you should love God, then follow me, [so] God will love you and forgive you your sins. And God is Forgiving and Merciful"* (Āl ʿImrān, 3:31).

Opposing the Messenger and choosing another path is misguidance. We must endeavour to be mindful not to deviate or become negligent (*ghafla*) of this imperative condition and instead operate within the framework of the divine oneness of God (*tawḥīd*), which is regarded as the hallmark of Muslim spirituality.

31 Aḥmad and al-Tirmidhī.

The Correct Manners of Making *Duʿāʾ*

- Perform ablutions (*wuḍū*)
- Praise God ﷻ and pray for the Messenger of God ﷺ before the *duʿāʾ*
- Raise one's hands
- Face the *qibla*
- Cry
- Expect the best from God ﷻ
- Complain only to God ﷻ
- Pray quietly
- Acknowledge one's sins
- Implore God earnestly
- Use the proper names and attributes of God ﷻ
- Repeat the *duʿāʾ* three times
- Begin by making *duʿāʾ* for oneself
- Pray for all Muslims
- Pray with concise *duʿāʾ*
- Say Āmīn
- Make *duʿāʾ* at all times
- Make *duʿāʾ* for all *ḥalāl* (permissible) matters
- Make *duʿāʾ* abundantly and consistently, especially when everything is going well
- Make *duʿāʾ* when one is in a likely condition of it being accepted

Factors that Contribute to the Acceptance of *Duʿāʾ*s

- Sincerity
- Expecting the best from God ﷻ
- Performing good deeds
- Fulfilling the rights of one's parents
- Making *duʿāʾ* at all times

- Performing voluntary acts after obligatory acts
- Repenting from sins
- Maintaining a humble and clean appearance
- Making *duʿāʾ* at holy places
- Adhering to the etiquette of *duʿāʾ*

Situations, States, and Places in which *Duʿāʾ*s are Accepted

- When remembering God constantly
- When reciting the Qurʾān
- When making *duʿāʾ* for a person in his absence
- The *duʿāʾ* of a just ruler
- During Ramaḍān
- During fasting
- On the Night of Decree (*laylat al-qadr*)
- When waking up at night
- In the last third of the night
- When the *adhān* is called
- Between the *adhān* and *iqāma*
- While reciting Sūrat al-Fātiḥa
- After the Sūrat al-Fātiḥa
- Before, during and after the *ṣalāt*
- During the prostration
- During battles (jihad)
- An hour on Friday
- After performing ablution (*wuḍū*)
- While performing *ḥajj*, *ʿumra,* especially, inside the Kaʿba, at al-Ṣafā and al-Marwa, while stoning the Jamarāt, on the day of Arafāt
- The first ten days of Dhū l-Ḥijja
- Before drinking Zamzam water
- By one who has been wronged
- By one in difficult circumstances

- After a calamity
- When travelling
- When making *duʿāʾ* at the crowing of a rooster
- While visiting the sick
- When sitting with someone dying
- When rain falls
- Before *ẓuhr*

Daily Remembrance (*Dhikr*) and Supplications

The Messenger of God ﷺ said, "The supplication of my brother Dhū Nūn (Prophet Yūnus ﷺ), who called on God while in the whale's belly: *There is no deity except You; exalted are You. Indeed, I have been of the wrongdoers* (al-Anbiyāʾ, 21:87)—no Muslim says it, for any situation whatsoever, except that God answers his call."[32] In another version it is mentioned, "...none who is experiencing difficulty employs it except that God relieves him of his difficulty."[33] This supplication includes both affirmation that God ﷻ alone has the right to be worshipped (*tawḥīd al-ilāhiyya*) and the acknowledgement of one's limitations and sins. This also includes a request for forgiveness.[34]

Sending prayers for the Messenger of God ﷺ is also a way to be rewarded for good deeds, relieve anguish, and distress, and shed sins simultaneously.[35] Daily recitations (*qirāʾa*) of the Qurʾān and reading the recommended morning and evening supplications (*adhkār al-ṣabaḥ wa-l-masāʾ*), including the ones read throughout the day and for different situations, are important ways of making daily connections

32 al-Tirmidhī, Aḥmad, and al-Nasāʾī.

33 al-Tirmidhī and al-Nasāʾī.

34 For a detailed exposition of this supplication refer to Ibn Taymiyya, *The Relief from Distress: An Explanation to the duʿāʾ of Yūnus.*

35 al-Tirmidhī.

with and asking for the protection and refuge (*istiʿādha*) of God ﷻ.[36] It is an instruction from God ﷻ that we remember and praise and glorify Him frequently (al-Aʿrāf, 7:205; al-Aḥzāb, 33:35, 41, 42). This daily remembrance is reciprocated by Him. God ﷻ mentions in the Qurʾān: *Therefore remember Me [by praising, glorifying]. I will remember you* (al-Baqara, 2:152).

By doing this we become successful (al-Jumʿa, 62:10) and our hearts most surely find rest (al-Raʿd, 13:28). When our lives become difficult, or we are in adverse conditions, the following words of Messenger of God ﷺ are a solace and further encouragement. Abū Hurayra ؓ reported that the Messenger of God ﷺ said: "Three people whose *duʿāʾ* will not be rejected are those who remember God often, the oppressed, and the just ruler."[37] Other than taking care of ourselves, visiting the sick and making *duʿāʾ* for them is also an immensely rewarding act. Abū Hurayra ؓ also reported that the Messenger of God ﷺ said: "When a man visits a [Muslim] brother [for God's sake], whether sick or well, God says, 'Good are you, and good is your walking. A place is secured for you in *janna*.'"[38] Upon his visit to the sick, he ﷺ would supplicate, saying, "O Lord of the people. In Your hand is the cure, and no one can remove the distress except You."[39] The Messenger of God ﷺ continued this by saying: "When you are present with a sick or dying person, say good things, because the angels endorse what you say with *āmīn*."[40] In the context of being afflicted by tests, trials, and tribulations, the Messenger of God ﷺ then reminds us that "Nothing repels predestination (*qadr*) except *duʿāʾ*."[41]

---

36 See Saʿeed al-Qahtaani, *Fortress of the Muslim: Invocations from the Qur'aan and Sunnah.*

37 al-Bayhaqī.

38 al-Tirmidhī, Ibn Māja, and others.

39 al-Bukhārī and Muslim.

40 Muslim, al-Bayhaqī, and others.

41 Ibn Ḥibbān.

Tests, Trials, and Afflictions

As believers, we all understand that afflictions, trials, and tests (*ibtilāʾ*), be they individually, in our families, health, property or wealth, are an inescapable part of our existence in this life. God ﷻ informs us that tests and trials are predestined for His creation:

> *And We will surely test you with something of fear and hunger and a loss of wealth and lives and fruits, but give good tidings to the patient, who, when disaster strikes them, say, "Indeed we belong to God, and indeed to Him we will return." Those are the ones upon whom are blessings from their Lord and mercy. And it is those who are the [rightly] guided* (al-Baqara, 2:155–157).

In Sūrat Āl ʿImrān (3:186), God ﷻ says: *You will surely be tested in your possessions and in yourselves.* And then as a staunch reminder in Sūrat al-ʿAnkabūt (29:2): *Do the people think that they will be left to say, 'We believe' and they will not be tried?*

In the prophetic traditions, it is reported by Abū Saʿid al-Khudrī ؓ that the Messenger of God ﷺ said: "When a believer is afflicted with hardship, sickness, worry, sadness, harm, or depression—even if it is something as trivial as a thorn's prick, God expiates some of his sins by it."[42] We also learn from the report of Abū Hurayra ؓ that the Messenger of God ﷺ said: "Affliction continues to befall believing men and women in their body, family, and property, until they meet God, burdened with no sin."[43] Additionally, Anas ؓ reported that the Messenger of God ﷺ said: "A reward's magnitude is according to the magnitude of the affliction. When God loves some people, He afflicts them. He who is content [with God's decree] will achieve [God's] acceptance, and he who

---

42 al-Bukhārī and Muslim.

43 Aḥmad, al-Tirmidhī, and others.

is discontent will attain [God's] anger."[44] We must then ask God ﷻ for success according to His decree (*qaḍā'*) and think well (*ḥusn al-ẓann*) of Him regardless of the outcome.

The Qur'ān and Sunna teach us to perceive tests and trials in the best of ways and derive maximum benefit from them. Tests are an opportunity to shed sins, multiply rewards, and ward off evil.[45] The believer understands that what was ordained to afflict him cannot miss him and what was ordained to miss him cannot afflict him. When we are then faced with afflictions, we should practise patience (*ṣabr*) and perseverance (*iḥtisāb*)[46] and look forward to rewards from God ﷻ. The Messenger of God ﷺ also reminds us that we should make *du'ā'* not only at difficult times, but also remember Him in the absence of it. He said, "The one who likes God to answer him at the time of adversity and hardship, then let him increase in *du'ā'* in times of ease."[47]

The Belief in God as Provider of Cures and Remedies

God ﷻ affirms His nearness in helping us:

> *And when My servants ask you, [O Muḥammad], concerning Me—indeed I am near. I respond to the invocation of the supplicant when he calls upon Me. So let them respond to Me [by obedience] and believe in Me that they may be [rightly] guided* (Ghāfir, 40:60).

We also learn from a report by Abū Hurayra ؓ that the Messenger of God ﷺ said: "There is no disease that God has sent down except that He has also sent down its treatment."[48] We must believe that God ﷻ

44 al-Tirmidhī,

45 Ibn Qayyim al-Jawziyya, *Provisions for the Hereafter (Mukhtaṣar Zād al-ma'ād).*

46 Ibn Qayyim al-Jawziyya, *al-Risālat al-tabukiyya.*

47 al-Tirmidhī and al-Ḥākim.

48 al-Bukhārī.

is the true healer and provider of a cure for our situation and predicament and that *duʿāʾ* is one important means that He has created for us to approach Him. One should strive to read *duʿāʾ* containing Qurʾānic verses with sincerity, conviction, and contemplation (al-Baqara, 2:242; Yūnus, 10:24; Yūsuf, 12:2, and Muḥammad, 47:24). According to Ibn Qayyim, "A medicine could be truly useful for a particular illness, but its effects would stop because of a patient's disbelief in it."[49] One must also strive to develop the qualities of a believer by being God-conscious (*taqwā*) and avoiding the prohibitions which undo our good deeds. God ﷻ informs us: *And whoever fears God and keeps his duty to Him, He will make a way for him to get out [from every difficulty]* (al-Ṭalaq, 65:2).

One must seek to develop a relationship with God ﷻ, putting complete confidence, reliance (*tawakkul*), and trust in Him. He commands His Messenger ﷺ: *So seek refuge with God [only]. Verily, it is He who is the all Hearing, the all Seeing* (Ghāfir, 40:46).

Our expectation of God ﷻ in helping, curing, and sustaining our health and life circumstances must be one of certainty and firmly rooted in our hearts and minds: as God ﷻ mentions, "I am as My servant thinks I am."[50] We must then supplicate to God ﷻ with certainty (*yaqīn*) that it will be answered, while understanding that God ﷻ does not accept the supplication of a person whose heart is negligent and inattentive.[51] We are reminded further about the wisdom of the way God ﷻ responses to our *duʿāʾ*; the Messenger of God ﷺ said: "No Muslim invokes with a supplication, but God answers his supplication, or delays it for him until the hereafter, or keeps him away from an equivalent evil."[52]

49 Ibn Qayyim al-Jawziyya, *Provisions for the Hereafter (Mukhtaṣar Zād al-maʿād).*

50 *Ḥadīth qudsī.*

51 al-Tirmidhī and al-Ḥākim.

52 al-Tirmidhī.

Ḥadīth Narrations on Qurʾānic Verses and *Sūras* as Supplications

The Messenger of God ﷺ endorsed the use of Sūrat al-Fātiḥa as an effective source of supplication and cure, as demonstrated in his praise of the companion, Abū Saʿīd ؓ, who used it as a cure for a Bedouin tribesman.[53] It was reported by Abū Hurayra ؓ in a *ḥadīth qudsī* that God ﷻ Himself directly responds to the supplicant with every verse read from Sūrat al-Fātiḥa.[54] The recital of *āyat al-kursī* (2:255) every morning and evening enables protection[55] and is also regarded as the best *āya* in the whole Qurʾān.[56] The protective effects of the last two *āya*s of Sūrat al-Baqara (2:285–286) has also been narrated by Abū Masʿūd al-Ansārī ؓ, who reported that the Messenger of God ﷺ said, "Whoever recites the two *āyāt* at the end of Sūrat al-Baqara at night, they suffice him [as protection for that night]."[57] These two verses contain eminent praise from God ﷻ for the Messenger of God ﷺ and his followers, while they contain beautiful supplication that God ﷻ teaches the believers. That is why they provide a protection from all harm and evil for those who recite them at night before sleeping. The last verses are also regarded as essential moral and spiritual resources to give us inner strength, courage, and patience required to live by all that al-Baqara teaches us.[58] Sūrat al-Baqara as a whole is regarded as an important source of protection against Satan and his evil. Abū Hurayra ؓ reported that the Messenger of God ﷺ said: "Do not turn your homes into graveyards [by not reciting the Qurʾān]. Indeed, Satan

---

53 al-Bukhārī, Muslim, and others.

54 Malik and others.

55 al-Bukhārī.

56 Muslim.

57 al-Bukhārī and Muslim.

58 Khurram Murad, *Key to al-Baqarah*.

is dispelled from a house in which Sūrat al-Baqara is recited."[59] The magicians who work to cast evil spells are also powerless against it.[60]

The Messenger of God ﷺ said, *Say, Qul huw-allāhu aḥad and the muʿawwidhatān* (al-Falaq 113 and al-Nās 114) three times in the evening and in the morning. This will protect you from all [harmful] things."[61] ʿUqba b. ʿĀmir al-Juhanī ؓ reported that the Messenger of God ﷺ told him: "O son of ʿĀbis should I not tell of what are best to use by those seeking protection? *Qul aʿūdhu bi-rabb al-falaq* and *Qul aʿūdhu bi-rabb al-nās*—these two *sūras*."[62] ʿĀʾisha ؓ reported: "When God's Messenger ﷺ went to bed, he would bring the palms of both his hands together, and breathe into them while reciting *Qul huwa Allāh aḥad; Qul aʿūdhu bi-rabb al-falaq; Qul aʿūdhu bi-rabb al-nās.* He would then rub them with whatever he could reach of his body, starting with his head, face, and the front part of his body. He would do this three times. When he was too ill, he asked me to do this for him." She also reported: "During the Prophet's ﷺ final sickness in which he passed away, he used to blow over himself with these *sūra*s of refuge. When he became very ill, I blew with them for him, rubbing over him with his own hand because of the blessing that is in it."[63] Abū Saʿīd al-Khudrī ؓ reported: "God's Messenger ﷺ used to seek [God's] protection from jinns and the evil eye of people [with various supplications] until the *muʿawwidhatān* were revealed. After that, he adhered to them and left all else."[64] The *muʿawwidhāt* (al-Ikhlaṣ 112, al-Falaq 113, and al-Nās 114) are referred to as the three *sūra*s of protection or refuge; they contain powerful words of praise for God ﷻ.[65]

---

59 Muslim and al-Tirmidhī.

60 Muslim.

61 Abū Dāwūd, al-Tirmidhī, and others.

62 al-Nasāʾī, Aḥmad, and others.

63 al-Bukhārī and Muslim.

64 al-Tirmidhī and Ibn Māja.

65 For further reading on this refer to Ibn Qayyim al-Jawziyya, *Tafseer*

Reasons for Reciting *Duʿāʾ*s from the Holy Qurʾān

In Sūrat al-Isrāʾ (17:82), God ﷻ affirms, *And We send down of the Qurʾān that which is healing and mercy for the believers, but it does not increase the wrongdoers except in loss.*

This verse is the framework for using the Qurʾānic verses as *duʿāʾ*. The Qurʾān, in its entirety, is both a cure and a mercy for us; a panacea for all our woes on earth. It is the only divine scripture that has been guarded and preserved by God himself (al-Nisāʾ, 4:48 and al-Ḥijr, 15:9). The reader of it is honoured with high rank in the hereafter[66] and the attentive listener receives mercy from God ﷻ (al-Aʿrāf, 7:204).[67] The powerful and transformative nature of the speech from God ﷻ is best reflected in Ibn Qayyim's statement in his *Zād al-maʿād*:

> Indeed, there is no medication for curing the heart more beneficent than the Qurʾān. It carries a complete remedy that would not leave any illness uncured. It would preserve the heart's well-being, and protect it completely from all harms... The superiority of the Lord of world's speech over other speeches is like God's superiority over His creation. His speech contains complete cure, beneficent protection, guiding light, and prevalent mercy. If this speech were to be sent down over a mountain, the mountain would collapse from its greatness and glory...[68]

Given the superiority, immediacy, and the special power in the words of the Qurʾān, how excellent then are these *duʿāʾ*s that come straight from our Lord? The Qurʾānic verses that are also *duʿāʾ*s, those read by

al-muʿawwidhatayn: The Explanation of Sūrah al-Falaq and Sūrah al-Nās.

66 Abū Dāwūd.

67 For further reading refer to Mahmood bin Ahmad bin Saaleh ad-Dausaree, *The Magnificence of the Qurʾān.*

68 Muhammad al-Jibāly, *Sickness, Regulations & Exhortations*, pp. 199 and 201.

believing men and women and by the prophets themselves—Adam, Noah, Abraham, Lot, Job, Shuʿayb, Jonah, Moses, David, Solomon, Zechariah, Jesus, and Muḥammad—have been carefully chosen for their general application and context. These prayers are extraordinarily relevant to and resonate with aspects of our emotional and social experiences today. By reaching out to God with gravity and sincerity, we can form a profound connection with Him and through these supplications call upon God's ﷻ intervention in our lives. One of the most universal and innate of human behaviours is the impulse to pray, to ask the Creator for help, for His pardon, relief, for His guidance, forgiveness, protection, support, and blessings. Prayer, whether spoken silently or aloud, alone or with others, has always been the core of spiritual wellness.

The Twofold Benefit of Qurʾānic *Duʿāʾ*s

1. They are a source by which we plead to God ﷻ for our needs.
2. We attain reward (*ḥasanāt*) for every letter we utter from them.

Accordingly, the Messenger of God ﷺ said, "Whoever reads a letter from God's book, he will be rewarded for it. And that reward will be multiplied by ten. I am not saying that 'alif, lām, mīm' is one letter, but 'alif' is a letter, 'lām' is a letter, and 'mīm' is a letter."[69] These *duʿāʾ* verses can be read by themselves, in conjunction with the *duʿāʾ*s from the Sunna or with personal words we use in our dialogue or intimate talk (*munājāt*) with God ﷻ. The accompanying CD contains all the Qurʾānic verses in the book to aid effective learning and memorisation.

May God ﷻ enable each of us to become the one who remembers (*dhākir*) to be close to the One remembered (*madhkūr*) and grant us

69 al-Tirmidhī.

the ability (*tawfiq*) in petitioning Him to answer our supplications and express our gratitude (*shukr*) for His timeless favours and blessings.

We thank God ﷻ for his generosity and giving us the opportunity to compile this book and pray that He will reward us all, abundantly, who have contributed to making this small work possible.

We would humbly ask those readers who derive any form of benefit from this work to remember us in your supplications.

Abul Hussain

Founding Director, ALIF RECORDINGS

London

February 2014

أدعية من القرآن الكريم

Duʿāʾ Verses from the Holy Qurʾān

Duʿāʾ Verses from the Holy Qurʾān

al-Fātiḥa, 1:1–7

بِسۡمِ ٱللَّهِ ٱلرَّحۡمَٰنِ ٱلرَّحِيمِ ﴿١﴾
ٱلۡحَمۡدُ لِلَّهِ رَبِّ ٱلۡعَٰلَمِينَ ﴿٢﴾
ٱلرَّحۡمَٰنِ ٱلرَّحِيمِ ﴿٣﴾ مَٰلِكِ يَوۡمِ ٱلدِّينِ ﴿٤﴾
إِيَّاكَ نَعۡبُدُ وَإِيَّاكَ نَسۡتَعِينُ ﴿٥﴾ ٱهۡدِنَا
ٱلصِّرَٰطَ ٱلۡمُسۡتَقِيمَ ﴿٦﴾ صِرَٰطَ ٱلَّذِينَ أَنۡعَمۡتَ
عَلَيۡهِمۡ غَيۡرِ ٱلۡمَغۡضُوبِ عَلَيۡهِمۡ
وَلَا ٱلضَّآلِّينَ ﴿٧﴾

In the name of God, the Entirely Merciful, the Especially Merciful. [All] praise is [due] to God, Lord of the worlds. The Entirely Merciful, the Especially Merciful. Sovereign of the Day of Recompense. It is You we worship and You we ask for help. Guide us to the straight path. The path of those upon whom You have bestowed favour, not of those who have evoked [Your] anger or of those who are astray.

al-Baqara, 2:127

رَبَّنَا تَقَبَّلْ مِنَّآ ۖ إِنَّكَ أَنتَ ٱلسَّمِيعُ ٱلْعَلِيمُ ﴿١٢٧﴾

Our Lord, accept [this] from us. Indeed You are the Hearing, the Knowing.

al-Baqara, 2:128

رَبَّنَا وَٱجْعَلْنَا مُسْلِمَيْنِ لَكَ وَمِن ذُرِّيَّتِنَآ أُمَّةً مُّسْلِمَةً لَّكَ وَأَرِنَا
مَنَاسِكَنَا وَتُبْ عَلَيْنَآ ۖ إِنَّكَ أَنتَ ٱلتَّوَّابُ ٱلرَّحِيمُ ﴿١٢٨﴾

Our Lord, and make us Muslims [in submission] to You and from our descendants a Muslim nation [in submission] to You. And show us our rites and accept our repentance. Indeed, You are the accepting of repentance, the Merciful.

al-Baqara, 2:201

رَبَّنَآ ءَاتِنَا فِى ٱلدُّنْيَا حَسَنَةً وَفِى ٱلْءَاخِرَةِ حَسَنَةً وَقِنَا عَذَابَ ٱلنَّارِ ﴿٢٠١﴾

Our Lord, give us in this world [that which is] good and in the hereafter [that which is] good and protect us from the punishment of the fire.

al-Baqara, 2:250

رَبَّنَآ أَفۡرِغۡ عَلَيۡنَا صَبۡرٗا وَثَبِّتۡ أَقۡدَامَنَا وَٱنصُرۡنَا عَلَى ٱلۡقَوۡمِ ٱلۡكَٰفِرِينَ ٢٥٠

Our Lord, pour upon us patience and plant our feet firmly and give us victory over the disbelieving people.

al-Baqara, 2:255

ٱللَّهُ لَآ إِلَٰهَ إِلَّا هُوَ ٱلۡحَيُّ ٱلۡقَيُّومُۚ لَا تَأۡخُذُهُۥ سِنَةٞ وَلَا نَوۡمٞۚ لَّهُۥ
مَا فِي ٱلسَّمَٰوَٰتِ وَمَا فِي ٱلۡأَرۡضِۗ مَن ذَا ٱلَّذِي يَشۡفَعُ عِندَهُۥٓ
إِلَّا بِإِذۡنِهِۦۚ يَعۡلَمُ مَا بَيۡنَ أَيۡدِيهِمۡ وَمَا خَلۡفَهُمۡۖ وَلَا يُحِيطُونَ
بِشَيۡءٖ مِّنۡ عِلۡمِهِۦٓ إِلَّا بِمَا شَآءَۚ وَسِعَ كُرۡسِيُّهُ ٱلسَّمَٰوَٰتِ
وَٱلۡأَرۡضَۖ وَلَا يَـُٔودُهُۥ حِفۡظُهُمَاۚ وَهُوَ ٱلۡعَلِيُّ ٱلۡعَظِيمُ ٢٥٥

God—there is no deity except Him, the Ever-Living, the Sustainer of [all] existence. Neither drowsiness overtakes Him nor sleep. To Him belongs whatever is in the heavens and whatever is on the earth. Who is it that can intercede with Him except by His permission? He knows what is [presently] before them and what will be after them, and they encompass not a thing of His knowledge except for what He wills. His *kursī* extends over the heavens and the earth, and their preservation tires Him not. And He is the Most High, the Most Great.

al-Baqara, 2:285–286

ءَامَنَ ٱلرَّسُولُ بِمَآ أُنزِلَ إِلَيۡهِ مِن رَّبِّهِۦ وَٱلۡمُؤۡمِنُونَۚ كُلٌّ ءَامَنَ بِٱللَّهِ
وَمَلَٰٓئِكَتِهِۦ وَكُتُبِهِۦ وَرُسُلِهِۦ لَا نُفَرِّقُ بَيۡنَ أَحَدٖ مِّن رُّسُلِهِۦۚ وَقَالُواْ
سَمِعۡنَا وَأَطَعۡنَاۖ غُفۡرَانَكَ رَبَّنَا وَإِلَيۡكَ ٱلۡمَصِيرُ ٢٨٥ لَا يُكَلِّفُ ٱللَّهُ نَفۡسًا
إِلَّا وُسۡعَهَاۚ لَهَا مَا كَسَبَتۡ وَعَلَيۡهَا مَا ٱكۡتَسَبَتۡۗ رَبَّنَا لَا تُؤَاخِذۡنَآ
إِن نَّسِينَآ أَوۡ أَخۡطَأۡنَاۚ رَبَّنَا وَلَا تَحۡمِلۡ عَلَيۡنَآ إِصۡرٗا كَمَا حَمَلۡتَهُۥ عَلَى
ٱلَّذِينَ مِن قَبۡلِنَاۚ رَبَّنَا وَلَا تُحَمِّلۡنَا مَا لَا طَاقَةَ لَنَا بِهِۦۖ وَٱعۡفُ عَنَّا
وَٱغۡفِرۡ لَنَا وَٱرۡحَمۡنَآۚ أَنتَ مَوۡلَىٰنَا فَٱنصُرۡنَا عَلَى ٱلۡقَوۡمِ ٱلۡكَٰفِرِينَ ٢٨٦

The Messenger has believed in what was revealed to him from his Lord, and [so have] the believers. All of them have believed in God and His angels and His books and His messengers, [saying], "We make no distinction between any of His messengers." And they say, "We hear and we obey. [We seek] Your forgiveness, our Lord, and to You is the [final] destination." God does not charge a soul except [with that within] its capacity. It will have [the consequence of] what [good] it has gained, and it will bear [the consequence of] what [evil] it has earned. "Our Lord, do not impose blame upon us if we have forgotten or erred. Our Lord, and lay not upon us a burden like that which You laid upon those before us. Our Lord, and burden us not with that which we have no ability to bear. And pardon us; and forgive us; and have mercy upon us. You are our protector, so give us victory over the disbelieving people."

Āl ʿImrān, 3:8

رَبَّنَا لَا تُزِغْ قُلُوبَنَا بَعْدَ إِذْ هَدَيْتَنَا وَهَبْ لَنَا
مِن لَّدُنكَ رَحْمَةً ۚ إِنَّكَ أَنتَ ٱلْوَهَّابُ ﴿٨﴾

Our Lord, let not our hearts deviate after You have guided us and grant us from Yourself mercy. Indeed, You are the Bestower.

Āl ʿImrān, 3:9

رَبَّنَآ إِنَّكَ جَامِعُ ٱلنَّاسِ لِيَوْمٍ لَّا رَيْبَ فِيهِ ۚ إِنَّ ٱللَّهَ لَا يُخْلِفُ ٱلْمِيعَادَ ﴿٩﴾

Our Lord, surely You will gather the people for a Day about which there is no doubt. Indeed, God does not fail in His promise.

Āl ʿImrān, 3:16

رَبَّنَآ إِنَّنَآ ءَامَنَّا فَٱغْفِرْ لَنَا ذُنُوبَنَا وَقِنَا عَذَابَ ٱلنَّارِ ﴿١٦﴾

Our Lord, indeed we have believed, so forgive us our sins and protect us from the punishment of the fire.

Āl ʿImrān, 3:26–27

قُلِ ٱللَّهُمَّ مَـٰلِكَ ٱلْمُلْكِ تُؤْتِى ٱلْمُلْكَ مَن تَشَآءُ وَتَنزِعُ ٱلْمُلْكَ مِمَّن
تَشَآءُ وَتُعِزُّ مَن تَشَآءُ وَتُذِلُّ مَن تَشَآءُ ۖ بِيَدِكَ ٱلْخَيْرُ ۖ إِنَّكَ عَلَىٰ كُلِّ شَىْءٍ
قَدِيرٌ ﴿٢٦﴾ تُولِجُ ٱلَّيْلَ فِى ٱلنَّهَارِ وَتُولِجُ ٱلنَّهَارَ فِى ٱلَّيْلِ ۖ وَتُخْرِجُ ٱلْحَىَّ مِنَ
ٱلْمَيِّتِ وَتُخْرِجُ ٱلْمَيِّتَ مِنَ ٱلْحَىِّ ۖ وَتَرْزُقُ مَن تَشَآءُ بِغَيْرِ حِسَابٍ ﴿٢٧﴾

Say, "O God, Owner of Sovereignty, You give sovereignty to whom You will and You take sovereignty away from whom You will. You honour whom You will and You humble whom You will. In Your hand is [all] good. Indeed, You are competent over all things. You cause the night to enter the day, and You cause the day to enter the night; and You bring the living out of the dead, and You bring the dead out of the living. And You give provision to whom You will without account [i.e., limit or measure]."

Āl ʿImrān, 3:38

رَبِّ هَبْ لِى مِن لَّدُنكَ ذُرِّيَّةً طَيِّبَةً ۖ إِنَّكَ سَمِيعُ ٱلدُّعَآءِ ﴿٣٨﴾

My Lord, grant me from Yourself a good offspring. Indeed, You are the Hearer of supplication.

Āl ʿImrān, 3:53

رَبَّنَآ ءَامَنَّا بِمَآ أَنزَلۡتَ وَٱتَّبَعۡنَا ٱلرَّسُولَ فَٱكۡتُبۡنَا مَعَ ٱلشَّٰهِدِينَ ٥٣

Our Lord, we have believed in what You revealed and have followed the messenger [i.e., Jesus], so register us among the witnesses [to truth].

Āl ʿImrān, 3:147

رَبَّنَا ٱغۡفِرۡ لَنَا ذُنُوبَنَا وَإِسۡرَافَنَا فِيٓ أَمۡرِنَا وَثَبِّتۡ
أَقۡدَامَنَا وَٱنصُرۡنَا عَلَى ٱلۡقَوۡمِ ٱلۡكَٰفِرِينَ ١٤٧

Our Lord, forgive us our sins and the excess [committed] in our affairs and plant our feet firmly and give us victory over the disbelieving people.

Āl ʿImrān, 3:191

رَبَّنَا مَا خَلَقۡتَ هَٰذَا بَٰطِلٗا سُبۡحَٰنَكَ فَقِنَا عَذَابَ ٱلنَّارِ ١٩١

Our Lord, You did not create this aimlessly; exalted are You [above such a thing]; then protect us from the punishment of the fire.

Āl ʿImrān, 3:192

رَبَّنَآ إِنَّكَ مَن تُدْخِلِ ٱلنَّارَ فَقَدْ أَخْزَيْتَهُۥ ۖ وَمَا لِلظَّـٰلِمِينَ مِنْ أَنصَارٍ ﴿١٩٢﴾

Our Lord, indeed whoever You admit to the fire—You have disgraced him, and for the wrongdoers there are no helpers.

Āl ʿImrān, 3:193

رَّبَّنَآ إِنَّنَا سَمِعْنَا مُنَادِيًا يُنَادِى لِلْإِيمَـٰنِ أَنْ ءَامِنُوا۟ بِرَبِّكُمْ فَـَٔامَنَّا ۚ
رَبَّنَا فَٱغْفِرْ لَنَا ذُنُوبَنَا وَكَفِّرْ عَنَّا سَيِّـَٔاتِنَا وَتَوَفَّنَا مَعَ ٱلْأَبْرَارِ ﴿١٩٣﴾

Our Lord, indeed we have heard a caller [i.e., Prophet Muḥammad] calling to faith, [saying], 'Believe in your Lord,' and we have believed. Our Lord, so forgive us our sins and remove from us our misdeeds and cause us to die with the righteous.

Āl ʿImrān, 3:194

رَبَّنَا وَءَاتِنَا مَا وَعَدتَّنَا عَلَىٰ رُسُلِكَ وَلَا تُخْزِنَا يَوْمَ
ٱلْقِيَـٰمَةِ ۗ إِنَّكَ لَا تُخْلِفُ ٱلْمِيعَادَ ﴿١٩٤﴾

Our Lord, and grant us what You promised us through Your messengers and do not disgrace us on the Day of Resurrection. Indeed, You do not fail in [Your] promise.

al-Nisāʾ, 4:75

رَبَّنَآ أَخْرِجْنَا مِنْ هَٰذِهِ ٱلْقَرْيَةِ ٱلظَّالِمِ أَهْلُهَا وَٱجْعَل لَّنَا
مِن لَّدُنكَ وَلِيًّا وَٱجْعَل لَّنَا مِن لَّدُنكَ نَصِيرًا ﴿٧٥﴾

Our Lord, take us out of this city of oppressive people and appoint for us from Yourself a protector and appoint for us from Yourself a helper.

al-Māʾida, 5:83

رَبَّنَآ ءَامَنَّا فَٱكْتُبْنَا مَعَ ٱلشَّٰهِدِينَ ﴿٨٣﴾

Our Lord, we have believed, so register us among the witnesses.

al-Aʿrāf, 7:23

رَبَّنَا ظَلَمْنَآ أَنفُسَنَا وَإِن لَّمْ تَغْفِرْ لَنَا وَتَرْحَمْنَا لَنَكُونَنَّ مِنَ ٱلْخَٰسِرِينَ ﴿٢٣﴾

Our Lord, we have wronged ourselves, and if You do not forgive us and have mercy upon us, we will surely be among the losers.

al-Aʿrāf, 7:47

رَبَّنَا لَا تَجْعَلْنَا مَعَ ٱلْقَوْمِ ٱلظَّٰلِمِينَ ﴿٤٧﴾

Our Lord, do not place us with the wrongdoing people.

al-Aʿrāf, 7:89

رَبَّنَا ٱفْتَحْ بَيْنَنَا وَبَيْنَ قَوْمِنَا بِٱلْحَقِّ وَأَنتَ خَيْرُ ٱلْفَٰتِحِينَ ﴿٨٩﴾

Our Lord, decide between us and our people in truth, and You are the best of those who give decision.

al-Aʿrāf, 7:126

رَبَّنَآ أَفْرِغْ عَلَيْنَا صَبْرًا وَتَوَفَّنَا مُسْلِمِينَ ﴿١٢٦﴾

Our Lord, pour upon us patience and let us die as Muslims [in submission to You].

al-Aʿrāf, 7:151

رَبِّ ٱغْفِرْ لِى وَلِأَخِى وَأَدْخِلْنَا فِى رَحْمَتِكَ ۖ وَأَنتَ أَرْحَمُ ٱلرَّٰحِمِينَ ﴿١٥١﴾

My Lord, forgive me and my brother and admit us into Your mercy, for You are the most merciful of the merciful.

al-Aʿrāf, 7:155–156

رَبِّ لَوْ شِئْتَ أَهْلَكْتَهُم مِّن قَبْلُ وَإِيَّٰىَ ۖ أَتُهْلِكُنَا بِمَا فَعَلَ ٱلسُّفَهَآءُ
مِنَّآ ۖ إِنْ هِىَ إِلَّا فِتْنَتُكَ تُضِلُّ بِهَا مَن تَشَآءُ وَتَهْدِى مَن تَشَآءُ ۖ
أَنتَ وَلِيُّنَا فَٱغْفِرْ لَنَا وَٱرْحَمْنَا ۖ وَأَنتَ خَيْرُ ٱلْغَٰفِرِينَ ﴿١٥٥﴾ وَٱكْتُبْ
لَنَا فِى هَٰذِهِ ٱلدُّنْيَا حَسَنَةً وَفِى ٱلْءَاخِرَةِ إِنَّا هُدْنَآ إِلَيْكَ... ﴿١٥٦﴾

My Lord, if You had willed, You could have destroyed them before and me [as well]. Would You destroy us for what the foolish among us have done? This is not but Your trial by which You send astray whom You will and guide whom You will. You are our Protector, so forgive us and have mercy upon us; and You are the best of forgivers. And decree for us in this world [that which is] good and [also] in the Hereafter; indeed, we have turned back to You.

al-Tawba, 9:129

حَسْبِىَ ٱللَّهُ لَآ إِلَٰهَ إِلَّا هُوَ ۖ عَلَيْهِ تَوَكَّلْتُ ۖ وَهُوَ رَبُّ ٱلْعَرْشِ ٱلْعَظِيمِ ﴿١٢٩﴾

Sufficient for me is God; there is no deity except Him. On Him I have relied, and He is the Lord of the Great Throne.

Yūnus, 10:85–86

رَبَّنَا لَا تَجْعَلْنَا فِتْنَةً لِّلْقَوْمِ ٱلظَّٰلِمِينَ ﴿٨٥﴾ وَنَجِّنَا
بِرَحْمَتِكَ مِنَ ٱلْقَوْمِ ٱلْكَٰفِرِينَ ﴿٨٦﴾

Our Lord, make us not [objects of] trial for the wrongdoing people. And save us by Your mercy from the disbelieving people.

Hud, 11:47

رَبِّ إِنِّيٓ أَعُوذُ بِكَ أَنْ أَسْـَٔلَكَ مَا لَيْسَ لِي بِهِۦ عِلْمٌ ۖ وَإِلَّا
تَغْفِرْ لِي وَتَرْحَمْنِيٓ أَكُن مِّنَ ٱلْخَٰسِرِينَ ﴿٤٧﴾

My Lord, I seek refuge in You from asking that of which I have no knowledge. And unless You forgive me and have mercy upon me, I will be among the losers.

Ibrāhīm, 14:38

رَبَّنَآ إِنَّكَ تَعْلَمُ مَا نُخْفِي وَمَا نُعْلِنُ ۗ وَمَا يَخْفَىٰ عَلَى
ٱللَّهِ مِن شَيْءٍ فِي ٱلْأَرْضِ وَلَا فِي ٱلسَّمَآءِ ﴿٣٨﴾

Our Lord, indeed You know what we conceal and what we declare, and nothing is hidden from God on the earth or in the heaven.

Ibrāhīm, 14:40

رَبِّ ٱجْعَلْنِى مُقِيمَ ٱلصَّلَوٰةِ وَمِن ذُرِّيَّتِى ۚ رَبَّنَا وَتَقَبَّلْ دُعَآءِ ﴿٤٠﴾

My Lord, make me an establisher of prayer, and [many] from my descendants. Our Lord, and accept my supplication.

Ibrāhīm, 14:41

رَبَّنَا ٱغْفِرْ لِى وَلِوَٰلِدَىَّ وَلِلْمُؤْمِنِينَ يَوْمَ يَقُومُ ٱلْحِسَابُ ﴿٤١﴾

Our Lord, forgive me and my parents and the believers the Day the account is established.

al-Isrāʾ, 17:24

رَبِّ ٱرْحَمْهُمَا كَمَا رَبَّيَانِى صَغِيرًا ﴿٢٤﴾

My Lord, have mercy upon them as they brought me up [when I was] small.

al-Isrāʾ, 17:80

رَبِّ أَدْخِلْنِى مُدْخَلَ صِدْقٍ وَأَخْرِجْنِى مُخْرَجَ صِدْقٍ
وَٱجْعَل لِّى مِن لَّدُنكَ سُلْطَٰنًا نَّصِيرًا ﴿٨٠﴾

My Lord, cause me to enter a sound entrance and to exit a sound exit and grant me from Yourself a supporting authority.

al-Kahf, 18:10

رَبَّنَآ ءَاتِنَا مِن لَّدُنكَ رَحۡمَةٗ وَهَيِّئۡ لَنَا مِنۡ أَمۡرِنَا رَشَدٗا ١٠

Our Lord, grant us from Yourself mercy and prepare for us from our affair right guidance.

Maryam, 19:4–5

رَبِّ إِنِّي وَهَنَ ٱلۡعَظۡمُ مِنِّي وَٱشۡتَعَلَ ٱلرَّأۡسُ شَيۡبٗا وَلَمۡ أَكُنۢ بِدُعَآئِكَ رَبِّ شَقِيّٗا ٤ وَإِنِّي خِفۡتُ ٱلۡمَوَٰلِيَ مِن وَرَآءِي وَكَانَتِ ٱمۡرَأَتِي عَاقِرٗا فَهَبۡ لِي مِن لَّدُنكَ وَلِيّٗا ٥

My Lord, indeed my bones have weakened, and my head has filled with white, and never have I been in my supplication to You, my Lord, unhappy [i.e., disappointed]. And indeed, I fear the successors after me, and my wife has been barren, so give me from Yourself an heir.

Ṭā-hā, 20:25–28

رَبِّ ٱشۡرَحۡ لِي صَدۡرِي ٢٥ وَيَسِّرۡ لِيٓ أَمۡرِي ٢٦ وَٱحۡلُلۡ عُقۡدَةٗ مِّن لِّسَانِي ٢٧ يَفۡقَهُواْ قَوۡلِي ٢٨

My Lord, expand [i.e. relax] for me my breast [with assurance]. And ease for me my task. And untie the knot from my tongue. That they may understand my speech.

Ṭā-hā, 20:114

رَّبِّ زِدْنِي عِلْمًا ﴿١١٤﴾

My Lord, increase me in knowledge.

al-Anbiyāʾ, 21:83

وَأَيُّوبَ إِذْ نَادَىٰ رَبَّهُۥٓ أَنِّي مَسَّنِيَ ٱلضُّرُّ وَأَنتَ أَرْحَمُ ٱلرَّٰحِمِينَ ﴿٨٣﴾

And [mention] Job, when he called to his Lord, "Indeed, adversity has touched me, and you are the Most Merciful of the merciful."

[When reading this verse as a personal supplication, it should only be read in the following way]

﴿ رَبِّ أَنِّي مَسَّنِيَ ٱلضُّرُّ وَأَنتَ أَرْحَمُ ٱلرَّٰحِمِينَ ﴾

al-Anbiyāʾ, 21:87

لَّآ إِلَٰهَ إِلَّآ أَنتَ سُبْحَٰنَكَ إِنِّي كُنتُ مِنَ ٱلظَّٰلِمِينَ ﴿٨٧﴾

There is no deity except You; exalted are You. Indeed, I have been of the wrongdoers.

al-Anbiyāʾ, 21:89

رَبِّ لَا تَذَرْنِي فَرْدًا وَأَنتَ خَيْرُ ٱلْوَٰرِثِينَ ﴿٨٩﴾

My Lord, do not leave me alone [with no heir], while You are the best of inheritors.

al-Anbiyāʾ, 21:112

رَبِّ ٱحْكُم بِٱلْحَقِّ ۗ وَرَبُّنَا ٱلرَّحْمَٰنُ ٱلْمُسْتَعَانُ عَلَىٰ مَا تَصِفُونَ ﴿١١٢﴾

My Lord, judge [between us] in truth. And our Lord is the Most Merciful, the one whose help is sought against that which you describe.

al-Muʾminūn, 23:29

رَبِّ أَنزِلْنِي مُنزَلًا مُّبَارَكًا وَأَنتَ خَيْرُ ٱلْمُنزِلِينَ ﴿٢٩﴾

My Lord, let me land at a blessed landing place, and You are the best to accommodate [us].

al-Muʾminūn, 23:94

رَبِّ فَلَا تَجْعَلْنِي فِي ٱلْقَوْمِ ٱلظَّٰلِمِينَ ﴿٩٤﴾

My Lord, then do not place me among the wrongdoing people.

al-Muʾminūn, 23:97–98

رَبِّ أَعُوذُ بِكَ مِنْ هَمَزَٰتِ ٱلشَّيَٰطِينِ ﴿٩٧﴾ وَأَعُوذُ بِكَ رَبِّ أَن يَحْضُرُونِ ﴿٩٨﴾

My Lord, I seek refuge in You from the incitements of the devils. And I seek refuge in You, my Lord, lest they be present with me.

al-Muʾminūn, 23:109

رَبَّنَآ ءَامَنَّا فَٱغْفِرْ لَنَا وَٱرْحَمْنَا وَأَنتَ خَيْرُ ٱلرَّٰحِمِينَ ﴿١٠٩﴾

Our Lord, we have believed, so forgive us and have mercy upon us, and You are the best of the merciful.

al-Muʾminūn, 23:118

رَبِّ ٱغْفِرْ وَٱرْحَمْ وَأَنتَ خَيْرُ ٱلرَّٰحِمِينَ ﴿١١٨﴾

My Lord, forgive and have mercy, and You are the best of the merciful.

al-Furqān, 25:65–66

رَبَّنَا ٱصْرِفْ عَنَّا عَذَابَ جَهَنَّمَ ۖ إِنَّ عَذَابَهَا كَانَ
غَرَامًا ﴿٦٥﴾ إِنَّهَا سَآءَتْ مُسْتَقَرًّا وَمُقَامًا ﴿٦٦﴾

Our Lord, avert from us the punishment of Hell. Indeed, its punishment is ever adhering. Indeed, it is evil as a settlement and residence.

al-Furqān, 25:74

رَبَّنَا هَبْ لَنَا مِنْ أَزْوَٰجِنَا وَذُرِّيَّٰتِنَا قُرَّةَ أَعْيُنٍ وَٱجْعَلْنَا لِلْمُتَّقِينَ إِمَامًا ﴿٧٤﴾

Our Lord, grant us from among our wives and offspring comfort to our eyes and make us a leader [i.e. example] for the righteous.

al-Shuʿarāʾ, 26:83–85

رَبِّ هَبْ لِى حُكْمًا وَأَلْحِقْنِى بِٱلصَّٰلِحِينَ ﴿٨٣﴾ وَٱجْعَل لِّى لِسَانَ
صِدْقٍ فِى ٱلْءَاخِرِينَ ﴿٨٤﴾ وَٱجْعَلْنِى مِن وَرَثَةِ جَنَّةِ ٱلنَّعِيمِ ﴿٨٥﴾

My Lord, grant me authority and join me with the righteous. And grant me a mention [i.e., reputation] of honour among later generations. And place me among the inheritors of the Garden of Pleasure.

al-Shuʿarāʾ, 26:169

رَبِّ نَجِّنِى وَأَهْلِى مِمَّا يَعْمَلُونَ ﴿١٦٩﴾

My Lord, save me and my family from [the consequence of] what they do.

al-Naml, 27:19

رَبِّ أَوْزِعْنِيٓ أَنْ أَشْكُرَ نِعْمَتَكَ ٱلَّتِيٓ أَنْعَمْتَ عَلَيَّ وَعَلَىٰ وَٰلِدَيَّ وَأَنْ
أَعْمَلَ صَٰلِحًا تَرْضَىٰهُ وَأَدْخِلْنِي بِرَحْمَتِكَ فِي عِبَادِكَ ٱلصَّٰلِحِينَ ﴿١٩﴾

My Lord, enable me to be grateful for Your favour which You have bestowed upon me and upon my parents and to do righteousness of which You approve. And admit me by Your mercy into [the ranks of] Your righteous servants.

al-Qaṣaṣ, 28:16

﴿رَبِّ إِنِّي ظَلَمْتُ نَفْسِي فَٱغْفِرْ لِي﴾ فَغَفَرَ
لَهُۥٓۚ إِنَّهُۥ هُوَ ٱلْغَفُورُ ٱلرَّحِيمُ ﴿١٦﴾

"My Lord, indeed I have wronged myself, so forgive me," and He forgave him. Indeed, He is the Forgiving, the Merciful.

[When reading this verse, the *duʿāʾ* part of it is shown between brackets.]

al-Qaṣaṣ, 28:17

رَبِّ بِمَآ أَنْعَمْتَ عَلَيَّ فَلَنْ أَكُونَ ظَهِيرًا لِّلْمُجْرِمِينَ ﴿١٧﴾

My Lord, for the favour You bestowed upon me, I will never be an assistant to the criminals.

al-Qaṣaṣ, 28:21

رَبِّ نَجِّنِى مِنَ ٱلْقَوْمِ ٱلظَّٰلِمِينَ ﴿٢١﴾

My Lord, save me from the wrongdoing people.

al-ʿAnkabūt, 29:30

رَبِّ ٱنصُرْنِى عَلَى ٱلْقَوْمِ ٱلْمُفْسِدِينَ ﴿٣٠﴾

My Lord, support me against the corrupting people.

al-Ṣāffāt, 37:100

رَبِّ هَبْ لِى مِنَ ٱلصَّٰلِحِينَ ﴿١٠٠﴾

My Lord, grant me [a child] from among the righteous.

Ghāfir, 40:7–9

رَبَّنَا وَسِعْتَ كُلَّ شَىْءٍ رَّحْمَةً وَعِلْمًا فَٱغْفِرْ لِلَّذِينَ تَابُوا۟ وَٱتَّبَعُوا۟ سَبِيلَكَ وَقِهِمْ عَذَابَ ٱلْجَحِيمِ ﴿٧﴾ رَبَّنَا وَأَدْخِلْهُمْ جَنَّٰتِ عَدْنٍ ٱلَّتِى وَعَدتَّهُمْ وَمَن صَلَحَ مِنْ ءَابَآئِهِمْ وَأَزْوَٰجِهِمْ وَذُرِّيَّٰتِهِمْ ۚ إِنَّكَ أَنتَ ٱلْعَزِيزُ ٱلْحَكِيمُ ﴿٨﴾ وَقِهِمُ ٱلسَّيِّـَٔاتِ ۚ وَمَن تَقِ ٱلسَّيِّـَٔاتِ يَوْمَئِذٍ فَقَدْ رَحِمْتَهُۥ ۚ وَذَٰلِكَ هُوَ ٱلْفَوْزُ ٱلْعَظِيمُ ﴿٩﴾

Our Lord, You have encompassed all things in mercy and knowledge, so forgive those who have repented and followed Your way and protect them from the punishment of Hellfire. Our Lord, and admit them to gardens of perpetual residence which You have promised them and whoever was righteous among their fathers, their spouses and their offspring. Indeed, it is You who is the Exalted in Might, the Wise. And protect them from the evil consequences [of their deeds]. And he whom You protect from evil consequences that Day—You will have given him mercy. And that is the great attainment.

al-Dukhān, 44:12

رَّبَّنَا ٱكْشِفْ عَنَّا ٱلْعَذَابَ إِنَّا مُؤْمِنُونَ ﴿١٢﴾

Our Lord, remove from us the torment; indeed, we are believers.

al-Aḥqāf, 46:15

رَبِّ أَوْزِعْنِيٓ أَنْ أَشْكُرَ نِعْمَتَكَ ٱلَّتِيٓ أَنْعَمْتَ عَلَيَّ
وَعَلَىٰ وَٰلِدَيَّ وَأَنْ أَعْمَلَ صَٰلِحًا تَرْضَىٰهُ وَأَصْلِحْ لِي فِي
ذُرِّيَّتِيٓۖ إِنِّي تُبْتُ إِلَيْكَ وَإِنِّي مِنَ ٱلْمُسْلِمِينَ ﴿١٥﴾

My Lord, enable me to be grateful for Your favour which You have bestowed upon me and upon my parents and to work righteousness of which You will approve and make righteous for me my offspring. Indeed, I have repented to You, and indeed, I am of the Muslims.

al-Ḥashr, 59:10

رَبَّنَا ٱغْفِرْ لَنَا وَلِإِخْوَٰنِنَا ٱلَّذِينَ سَبَقُونَا بِٱلْإِيمَٰنِ وَلَا تَجْعَلْ
فِي قُلُوبِنَا غِلًّا لِّلَّذِينَ ءَامَنُوا۟ رَبَّنَآ إِنَّكَ رَءُوفٌ رَّحِيمٌ ﴿١٠﴾

Our Lord, forgive us and our brothers who preceded us in faith and put not in our hearts [any] resentment toward those who have believed. Our Lord, indeed You are Kind and Merciful.

al-Mumtaḥana, 60:4

رَبَّنَا عَلَيْكَ تَوَكَّلْنَا وَإِلَيْكَ أَنَبْنَا وَإِلَيْكَ ٱلْمَصِيرُ ﴿٤﴾

Our Lord, upon You we have relied, and to You we have returned, and to You is the destination.

al-Mumtaḥana, 60:5

رَبَّنَا لَا تَجْعَلْنَا فِتْنَةً لِّلَّذِينَ كَفَرُوا۟ وَٱغْفِرْ لَنَا
رَبَّنَآ ۖ إِنَّكَ أَنتَ ٱلْعَزِيزُ ٱلْحَكِيمُ ۝٥

Our Lord, make us not [objects of] torment for the disbelievers and forgive us, our Lord. Indeed, it is You who is the Exalted in Might, the Wise.

al-Taḥrīm, 66:8

رَبَّنَآ أَتْمِمْ لَنَا نُورَنَا وَٱغْفِرْ لَنَآ ۖ إِنَّكَ عَلَىٰ كُلِّ شَىْءٍ قَدِيرٌ ۝٨

Our Lord, perfect for us our light and forgive us. Indeed, You are over all things competent.

Nūḥ, 71:26

رَّبِّ لَا تَذَرْ عَلَى ٱلْأَرْضِ مِنَ ٱلْكَٰفِرِينَ دَيَّارًا ۝٢٦

My Lord, do not leave upon the earth from among the disbelievers an inhabitant.

Nūḥ 71:28

رَّبِّ ٱغْفِرْ لِى وَلِوَٰلِدَىَّ وَلِمَن دَخَلَ بَيْتِىَ مُؤْمِنًا وَلِلْمُؤْمِنِينَ
وَٱلْمُؤْمِنَٰتِ وَلَا تَزِدِ ٱلظَّٰلِمِينَ إِلَّا تَبَارًۢا ﴿٢٨﴾

My Lord, forgive me and my parents and whoever enters my house a believer and the believing men and believing women. And do not increase the wrongdoers except in destruction.

al-Ikhlāṣ, 112:1–4

بِسْمِ ٱللَّهِ ٱلرَّحْمَٰنِ ٱلرَّحِيمِ
قُلْ هُوَ ٱللَّهُ أَحَدٌ ﴿١﴾ ٱللَّهُ ٱلصَّمَدُ ﴿٢﴾ لَمْ يَلِدْ وَلَمْ
يُولَدْ ﴿٣﴾ وَلَمْ يَكُن لَّهُۥ كُفُوًا أَحَدٌۢ ﴿٤﴾

In the Name of God, the Most Compassionate,
the Most Merciful.

Say, "He is God, [who is] One. God, the Eternal Refuge. He neither begets nor is born. Nor is there to Him any equivalent."

al-Falaq, 113:1–5

بِسۡمِ ٱللَّهِ ٱلرَّحۡمَٰنِ ٱلرَّحِيمِ

قُلۡ أَعُوذُ بِرَبِّ ٱلۡفَلَقِ ① مِن شَرِّ مَا خَلَقَ ② وَمِن شَرِّ غَاسِقٍ إِذَا وَقَبَ ③ وَمِن شَرِّ ٱلنَّفَّٰثَٰتِ فِي ٱلۡعُقَدِ ④ وَمِن شَرِّ حَاسِدٍ إِذَا حَسَدَ ⑤

In the Name of God, the Most Compassionate,
the Most Merciful.

Say, "I seek refuge in the Lord of daybreak. From the evil of that which He created. And from the evil of darkness when it settles. And from the evil of the blowers in knots. And from the evil of an envier when he envies."

al-Nās, 114:1–6

بِسۡمِ ٱللَّهِ ٱلرَّحۡمَٰنِ ٱلرَّحِيمِ

قُلۡ أَعُوذُ بِرَبِّ ٱلنَّاسِ ① مَلِكِ ٱلنَّاسِ ② إِلَٰهِ ٱلنَّاسِ ③ مِن شَرِّ ٱلۡوَسۡوَاسِ ٱلۡخَنَّاسِ ④ ٱلَّذِي يُوَسۡوِسُ فِي صُدُورِ ٱلنَّاسِ ⑤ مِنَ ٱلۡجِنَّةِ وَٱلنَّاسِ ⑥

In the Name of God, the Most Compassionate, the Most
Merciful.

Say, "I seek refuge in the Lord of mankind. The Sovereign of mankind. The God of mankind. From the evil of the retreating whisperer. Who whispers [evil] into the breasts of Mankind. From among the jinn and mankind."

اللّٰهُمَّ صَلِّ عَلٰى مُحَمَّدٍ وَعَلٰى آلِ مُحَمَّدٍ، كَمَا صَلَّيْتَ عَلٰى إِبْرَاهِيْمَ وَعَلٰى
آلِ إِبْرَاهِيْمَ، إِنَّكَ حَمِيْدٌ مَجِيْدٌ، اَللّٰهُمَّ بَارِكْ عَلٰى مُحَمَّدٍ وَعَلٰى آلِ مُحَمَّدٍ،
كَمَا بَارَكْتَ عَلٰى إِبْرَاهِيْمَ وَعَلٰى آلِ إِبْرَاهِيْمَ، إِنَّكَ حَمِيْدٌ مَجِيْدٌ.

O God, bless Muḥammad and the family of Muḥammad as you blessed Ibrahim and the family of Ibrahim, for Your are truly the Most Praiseworthy and Noble. O God, favour Muḥammad and the family of Muḥammad as You favoured Abraham and the family of Abraham, for You are truly Most Praiseworthy and Noble. (al-Bukhārī)

Recommended Reading

al-Albaani, Muhammad Nasir ud-Deen. *Tawassul: Its Types and Its Rulings*. Translated by Daawood ibn Ronald Burbank. Birmingham, UK: al-Hidaayah Publishing & Distribution, 1996.

Ameen, Abū l-Mundhir Khaleel ibn Ibraheem. *The Jinn & Human Sickness, Remedies in the Light of the Quraan & Sunnah*. Riyadh: Darussalam, 2005.

al-Awaaishah, Hassain. *The Book of Dua*. Translated by Abdul Ali A. Hamid. Edited by Abu Muntasir ibn Mohar Ali. Ipswich, UK: Jam'iat Ihyaa Minhaaj al-Sunnah, 1995.

Badawi, Jamal A. *Selected Prayers: A Collection of Du'a' from the Qur'an and Sunnah*. UK: Ta-Ha Publications, 2006.

al-Bukhārī, Muḥammad b. Ismāʿīl. *al-Adab al-mufrad: A Code for Everyday Living, the Example of the Early Muslims*. Leicester, UK: Islamic Academy, 1990.

———. *The Translation of the Meanings of Sahih al-Bukhārī*. 9 vols. Translated by Muhammad Muhsin Khan. Riyadh: Darussalam, 1997.

ad-Dausaree, Mahmood bin Aḥmad bin Saaleh. *The Magnificence of the Qurʾān*. Riyadh: Darussalam, 2006.

al-Essa, Waled K. S. *Authentic Supplications of the Prophet*. Kissimmee, Florida: Daar of Islamic Heritage, 1993.

Ibn Kathīr. *Tafsīr Ibn Kathīr*. Abridged vols. 1–10. Riyadh: Darussalam, 2000.

Ibn Qayyim al-Jawziyya. *al-Fawāʾid: A Collection of Wise Sayings*. Translated by Bayan Translation Service. Mansoura, Egypt: Umm Al-Qura Publishing & Distribution, 2004.

———. *Iʿlām al-muwwaqiʿīn*. Edited by Iṣṣām al-Dīn al-Sabābitī. Cairo: Dār al-Ḥadīth, 2006.

———. *The Invocation of God.* [al-Wābil al-Ṣayyib min al-Kalim al-Ṭayyib]. Translated by Michael Abdurrahman Fitzgerald and Moulay Youssef Slitine. Cambridge: Islamic Texts Society, 2000.

———. *Patience and Gratitude: An abridged translation of ʿUddat al-ṣābirīn wa-dhakhīrat al-shākirīn.* London: Ta-Ha Publishers, 1997.

———. *Provisions for the Hereafter (Mukhtaṣar zād al-maʿād).* Riyadh: Darussalam, 2003.

———. *al-Risālat al-tabukiyya: The Spiritual Journey to Allāh & His Messenger.* Translated by Muhammad Mustafa al-Jibāly. Beirut: al-Kitāb al-Sunna Publishing, 2007.

———. *Tafseer al-muʿawwidhatayn: The Explanation of Sūrah al-Falaq and Sūrah al-Nas.* Translated by AbdAllāh Elaceri. London: al-Firdouse, 2005.

Ibn Taymiyya. *Ibn Taymiyyah's Essay on Servitude.* Translated by Abu Safwan Farid ibn Abdulwaahid Haibatan. Birmingham, UK: al-Hidaayah Publishing and Distribution, 1999.

———. *Kitāb al-Īmān: The Book of Emaan According to the Classical Work of Shaikh ul-Islam Ibn Taymiyyah.* Translated by Dr. Muhammad Naim Yasin. London: al-Firdouse, 1997.

———. *The Noble Words: Remembrance and Prayers of the Prophet Muhammad by Ibn Taymiya.* [al-Kalim al-ṭayyib]. Translated by Suad bint Mufti Iqbal Ahmad Azami. Leicester, UK: Islamic Academy, 2003.

———. *The Relief from Distress: An Explanation to the duʿāʾ of Yūnus.* Birmingham, UK: Daar Us-Sunnah Publishers, 2006.

———. *al-Wāsiṭa bayn al-ḥaqq wa-l-khālq: The Meditation Between al-Ḥaqq Allāh and the Creation.* Translated by Aboo Iyaad and Amjad bin Muhammad Rafiq. Edited by Muhammad bin Jameel Zayno. Walthamstow, UK: Invitation to Islam, 1998.

al-Jibāly, Muhammad Mustafā. *The Dreamer's Handbook: Sleep Etiquettes & Dream Interpretation in Light of the Sunnah.*

General Index